Judy Buswell © 1995

For

....

From

....

Date

....

'tis the Season

Illustrated by *Judy Buswell*

Brownlow

Little Treasures Miniature Books

75 Ways to Spoil Your Grandchild

A Little Book of Love

A Little Cup of Tea

A Little Nest of Pleasant Thoughts

Baby's First Little Book

Baby Oh Baby • Beside Still Waters

Catch of the Day

Dear Daughter • Dear Teacher

For My Secret Pal

Friends · Grandmothers

Grandmothers are for Loving

Happiness is Homemade

How Does Your Garden Grow?

Little Book of Blessings

Mom, I Love You

My Sister, My Friend

Quiet Moments of Inspiration

Quilted Hearts · Roof With a View

Seasons of Friendship

Sisters · Tea Time Friends

They Call It Golf · 'Tis the Season

A Season of Traditions & Memories

A Child's Memory of Christmas

Christmas Eve finally came and we could open presents. "Every available relative" (as Charles

Dickens put it) was there, but no gifts could be opened before the "program." My cousins and I always had to sing Christmas carols, and the holly-jolly type like "Jingle Bells" just would not do. They wanted the old familiar religious carols of shepherds and sheep, Baby Jesus and the manger. One year we ended up singing the first verse of "Joy to the World" five times in a row because we couldn't remember the other verses, or any other song on the approved list. The presents were next, and while small, were most lovingly given and received.

PAUL C. BROWNLOW

The modern tradition of hanging stockings by the fire came from a legend that tells of the kind and generous St. Nicholas who wanted to give money to a poor family. He dropped the money down the chimney and it rolled into a stocking that had fallen to the floor nearby. The family found it the next morning.

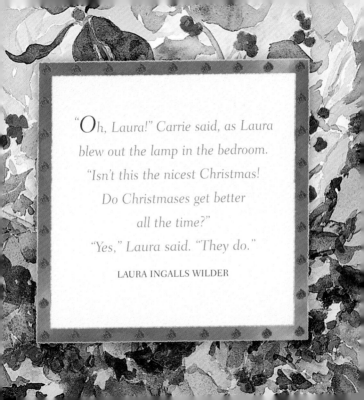

"Oh, Laura!" Carrie said, as Laura
blew out the lamp in the bedroom.
"Isn't this the nicest Christmas!
Do Christmases get better
all the time?"
"Yes," Laura said. "They do."

LAURA INGALLS WILDER

The Christmas Flower

*A*mong Christmas traditions, the poinsettia is relatively new. In 1825, Joel Roberts Poinsett of

Charleston found the flaming, star-shaped blossom growing wild on the hillsides of Mexico. The locals called them "Flowers of the Holy Night" and used them in Nativity celebrations. While serving as the first American ambassador to Mexico, Poinsett sent plantings of the blossom back to South Carolina and introduced the Christmas Flower to America.

The First Bike

I'll never forget the Christmas that my brother got his first bike. Of course we all went outside and watched as my Dad taught him how to ride it. Dad held on to the seat and the handlebars and ran, pushing my brother down the road in front of our house. The unfortunate thing was that Dad forgot to teach him the fine art of braking. Mark was resourceful, though. He carefully steered the bike under a large oak tree and grabbed the limb as he went under — the bike kept going while my brother dropped safely to the ground. It was months before we could convince him that using the brakes was truly the better way of stopping.

MELISSA REAGAN

Oranges at Christmas

As early as I can remember,
my dad and I would always eat
oranges together at Christmastime.
He would carefully peel the big juicy
fruit, and I would wait patiently for
him to give me my share. We would
soon finish one and with a smile
and a knowing look, it was off to
the kitchen for just one more.

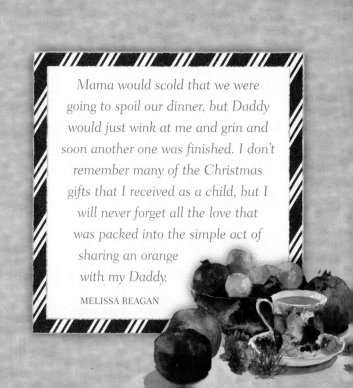

*Mama would scold that we were
going to spoil our dinner, but Daddy
would just wink at me and grin and
soon another one was finished. I don't
remember many of the Christmas
gifts that I received as a child, but I
will never forget all the love that
was packed into the simple act of
sharing an orange
with my Daddy.*

MELISSA REAGAN

A Season of
Peace &
Goodwill

Silent night, holy night!
All is calm, all is bright

Round yon Virgin
Mother and Child,

Holy Infant so
tender and mild!

Sleep in heavenly peace,

Sleep in heavenly peace.

JOSEPH MOHR & FRANZ GRUBER

The simple things
that bless our fireside,

The peace and joy we shared,
the love sublime,

The heritage of home
at Christmastime!

E. SHERMAN SMITH

What is Christmas?
It is tenderness for the past,
courage for the present,
hope for the future. It is a fervent
wish that every cup may overflow
with blessings rich and eternal,
and that every path may lead to peace.

AGNES M. PHARO

A Quiet Peace

Every Christmas Eve,
when it is late, I try to
walk outside briefly and listen
to the peaceful quiet.
From my hillside, I can see
twinkling lights for miles
in every direction.

It is cold and the air is crisp.
The busy, hectic pace of getting
ready for Christmas is finally over.
Families are bundled into their
homes together. Even the dogs are
asleep. And for a few minutes,
the peace of the season surrounds
me and renews my spirit.

PAUL C. BROWNLOW

Song of the Thrush

I heard a bird sing
In the dark
of December
A magical thing
And sweet
to remember.

OLIVER HERFORD

A Season of

Light &

Life

Christmas Every Day

What if we could spread out the
spirit of Christmas a little each day?
What if everyday life could be tinged
with just a touch more generosity and
kindness, tenderness and love?
Wouldn't that be the real legacy
of Christmas we are longing for?

Two Lights

On one dark night in Bethlehem,
two lights were born. One star shone
gloriously bright in the eastern sky and
pointed the way to a baby lying in a manger.
But the baby was a light that outshone
even the star that announced His birth
and His light would forever shine the
way to the Father in heaven.

*W*hen they saw the star,
they were overjoyed.

MATTHEW 2:10

*T*he light that shines from
the humble manger is
strong enough to lighten our
way to the end of our days.

AUTHOR UNKNOWN

When Hope
Was Born

Rise, happy morn, rise holy morn,
Draw forth the cheerful day from night;
O Father, touch the East, and light
The light that shone
when Hope was born.

ALFRED, LORD TENNYSON

And they traveled by night and they slept by day. For their guide was a beautiful, wonderful star.

HENRY WADSWORTH LONGFELLOW

Star of Wonder

O Star of wonder,

Star of night,

Star of royal beauty bright,

Westward leading,

Still proceeding,

Guide us to Thy perfect Light!

JOHN HENRY HOPKINS, JR.

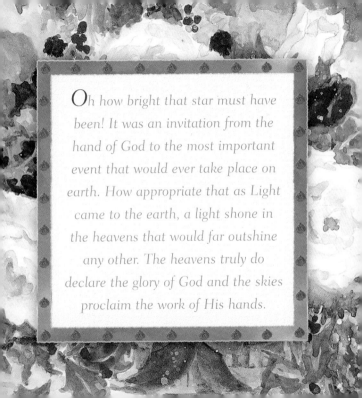

Oh how bright that star must have
been! It was an invitation from the
hand of God to the most important
event that would ever take place on
earth. How appropriate that as Light
came to the earth, a light shone in
the heavens that would far outshine
any other. The heavens truly do
declare the glory of God and the skies
proclaim the work of His hands.

A Season of

Joy &

Giving

Gift of Joy

Somehow not only
for Christmas
but all the
long year through,
The joy that
you give others
is the joy that
comes back to you.

JOHN GREENLEAF WHITTIER

The magi of the East, in sandals worn,

Knelt reverent, sweeping round,

With long pale beards,

their gifts upon the ground,

The incense, myrrh, and gold.

ELIZABETH BARRETT BROWNING

The heart of the giver

makes the gift dear and precious.

MARTIN LUTHER

Joy to the world, the Lord is come!

Let earth receive her King;

Let ev'ry heart prepare Him room

And heav'n and nature sing,

And heav'n and nature sing,

And heav'n and heav'n and nature sing.

ISAAC WATTS

Christmas is more than a gift-laden tree,

It is caring and sharing... unselfishly.

LAURA BAKER HAYNES

The finest Christmas gift is not the one that costs the most money, but the one that carries the most love.

HENRY VAN DYKE

If you have love in your heart you will always have something to give.

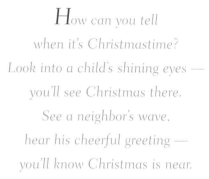

*H*ow can you tell
when it's Christmastime?
Look into a child's shining eyes —
you'll see Christmas there.
See a neighbor's wave,
hear his cheerful greeting —
you'll know Christmas is near.